Job

Olwyn Harris

Reflections around the life of Job
who suffered in the storm,
and found The Lord as his peace.

Suitable for Individual and Group Discussion

Copyright © Olwyn Harris 2025

ISBN   Softcover   978-1-923021-44-0
       eBook   978-1-923021-45-7

All rights reserved. No part of this book may be reproduced or transmitted in any form or by any means, electronic, or mechanical, including photocopying, recording or by any information storage and retrieval system without the permission in writing by the copyright owner.
Unless otherwise stated Scriptures quoted here are from the King James Version (Authorised version). First published in 1611. Quoted from the KJV Classic Reference Bible, copyright 1983 by the Zondervan Corporation.

Published by: Reading Stones Publishing
Helen Brown & Wendy Wood
Woodwendy1982.wixsite.com/readingstones
Cover Design: Olwyn Harris
Dinosaur- https://pixabay.com/photos/dinosaur-primeval-times-lizards-4475295/ Artist: Frank_P_AJJ74
Dragon- https://pixabay.com/photos/iguana-lizard-dragon-reptile-4457653/ Artist - Akiroq

For more copies contact the publisher at:
Glenburnie
212 Glenburnie Road
ROB ROY NSW 2360
Mobile: 0422 577 663
Email: Readingstonespublishing@gmail.com

Acknowledgement:

My heartfelt appreciation to Pastor Dawn Peel, emeritus, who has held a role as part of the credentialing of pastors within the ACC church. Thank you for your willingness to cast your theological eye over these chapters.

Table of Contents

Job

Table of Contents 5

Introduction 7

Introducing Job and the problem of suffering 9

The Problem of Supporting others in Suffering 25

The Problem of a Legal Lens 39

The Problem of Projecting 51

The Problem of Not Listening 56

The Problem of Spiritualising 66

The Problem of God's Sovereignty 81

Endnotes 97

Introduction

Taking time to reflect on the stories in the Bible, is something that we are encouraged to do in our walk with Jesus. I don't know anyone who would suggest this is not an important aspect of being a disciple of Jesus. Yet I have noticed, over and over, there is a widespread illiteracy regarding the stories in the Bible which I grew up with. I've also noticed that this unfamiliarity is not restricted to new Christians. I suspect we are more comfortable with the popular narratives on our TV streaming service, than the ones in our Bible.

The Holy Spirit, in his wisdom, has chosen the platform of storytelling as one way to communicate our spiritual relationship him, packed with wisdom, truth, morality, and values. It is not the only way God speaks to us, yet so much practical wisdom can be distilled from these narratives. Our challenge is how to access these stories in a way that allows them to be understandable in a world that is so far removed from the times when these accounts occurred. This series on *Reflections in the Bible* is not intended to be an exercise in theological exegesis, rather to create an opportunity to explore some of these stories. It is an invitation to go on a journey of reflection around what is described. What can we distil from these life-stories that makes sense for us today? Some of these narratives may be familiar. Some of them may be forgotten. Some of them are hard to understand. This is an opportunity to take time to slow down, invite the Holy Spirit to whisper his insight as we explore some of the stories he has preserved for us.

This book is intended to be a reflective space to use alongside your Bible. Sometimes, even the act of opening the pages of our Bible can be a challenge. So, open up! Don't skip over the suggested passages marked as "Bible Readings". The scriptures tagged as "Bible Reference" are intended to bookmark passages, if you want to check them. Take hold of the opportunity to read or revisit God's Word. You are invited to use these pages as a place to scribble in margins; explore your own questions; and use reflective prompts to go a little deeper. My prayer is that it will be a springboard to explore the incredible love story of God, his great good news of redemption and His grace will draw you closer to who He is as our Good Father. I trust it moves each of us to appreciate more about our relationship with God, ourselves and life in community.

I
Introducing Job and the problem of suffering

In this collection of reflections, we are going to have a look at this book of Job.

I was talking to a lady who had been diagnosed with breast cancer, and her journey through her treatment was harrowing and difficult.
She said that she had found it so hard to find comfort from those around her... and it was also difficult for her to reconcile her faith during this season in her life...
But she said something I have never forgotten... "You know... I have been comforted most by reading the book of Job. It is not a book I would have thought would speak to me, but I have read it over and over again..."

It was not the inspirational quotes, or the motivational sermons, or the positive affirmations that ministered comfort... but a book from the Bible with a very short name.

And it sits right in the middle of our bible... the book of Job.

Wisdom Literature

The Book of Job sits within the Wisdom and Poetry section of the Library of the Bible. Not only that, but it is also a book that has been given many stunning literary reviews over the years:

> "The Book of Job, book of Hebrew scripture that is often counted among the masterpieces of world literature.[i]
> "The Book of Job is one of the literary masterpieces of all time..."[ii]
> "The Book of Job is one of the most celebrated pieces of biblical literature, not only because it explores some of the most profound questions humans ask about their lives, but also because it is extremely well written."[iii]

Doesn't that make you a little bit curious? Yet this is a book that I don't often delve into. It seems dark and the subject of suffering is not one I am naturally drawn to. I visit suffering every day with people I work with... I don't necessarily want it to be part of my devotional experience as well. But the reality is... this is a topic that impacts us all... whether at work, or at home... or in our private spaces. This problem of pain is a reality of everyday life.

So, if God... in his wisdom, has placed this book... in the section of Wisdom Literature in our scriptures... then perhaps there is some *wisdom* that we can acquire here, that will support our own treatment and understanding of the reality of pain. So, I invite you to join me as we have a look at who Job was.

An ancient dramatic play

The book of Job is unique in that it is written as a theatrical play. The characters in the play are given large, wordy monologues. It is poetic in its structure. It is written in such a way, where one character says his piece and Job has the right of reply. Back and forth; back and forth. In many ways, it has the feel of a legal or courtroom drama.

When this book was written is unknown, but it is generally accepted that it is dated as the most ancient of all the writings in the bible. There are some markers in the text that suggest it was written during the time of Abraham... and it is possible that Abraham was one of Job's contemporaries.

A portrait of dealing with pain...

The subject of this piece is exploring the profound questions of life, and rather than giving philosophical answers to these questions, the playwright explores these ideas through the eyes of the main character Job. Job is a good man.
He is a wealthy man. An influential man.
A godly man. A family man.
And bad stuff... *extreme* stuff... happens to him.
And the question that screams off the stage... is "Why!?"
Why would God allow it?
Why does bad stuff happen to good people?
Where is the goodness of God, where is the justice?
Where is the comfort in pain?
How do we make sense of the awful realities that we see around us?

A 'biopic' in the Wisdom-Poetic section

The fact that the Book of Job is written in the format of a play and sits in the poetry section of the Bible becomes a problem for some people, because the question that arises is: Is this play about a real person... or is it just some fictional story? After all, it sits beside other poetry.

Perhaps you already some of definite ideas about whether Job was an actual person or not. I have reasons to think that Job was an historical figure. But for some people it is enough that the truth within this book is like a parable, a story that is told to unpack some of the profound questions of life. Jesus told parables all the time. Storytelling was a device that he used frequently in his teaching. The message of the Good Samaritan is no less profound, just because Jesus made him up as a fictional character to teach a spiritual truth.

But I don't think it has to be one or the other – either/or. I like to think of the book of Job... the theatre of the play... as a Biopic. A biopic is a play or a movie, based on a real person and real events. That biopic remembers and honours a real person and their story... and explores it through theatre.

What movies have you seen that were about a real person?

Did you think that because their story was dramatized, that the person didn't actually exist?

We know that actors play the parts. We know that there are creative elements introduced for the sake of art.

I saw the movie Machine Gun Preacher[iv] once. The lead role was played by Gerard Butler. Great portrayal. But when I met Sam Childers... the actual Machine Gun Preacher, there was nothing fictional about him or his story. As he told his own story, I could see creative elements that were introduced to make the movie sit on the silver screen. He didn't look like a Hollywood Gerard Butler, but Sam's take on his life-story being made into an artistic portrayal – a movie... was that... first and foremost... it got people talking! It opened doors into discussions about God that hadn't happen before. Sam spoke about pubs he'd been to, that just ran his movie on a loop instead of the standard erotic music videos... and the conversations about God, and social justice, that movie generated could not be counted. For him, this format had its purpose.

I wonder if the format of the book of Job has a similar purpose. I wonder if it could generate some conversations around God and circumstances, and how the painful things that we experience might fit into our meaning-making about life.

Bible Reading
Job 1:1

Job, was he a real person?

Job was a man from the land of Uz. So how did I come to the conclusion that the book of Job was based on a real person? As we open up the book of Job we are immediately introduced to the main character. This is the way the stage is set as the curtain opens: *In the land of Uz.* (Not to be confused with the Land of Oz and the Emerald city!) This is pointing to a specific place in Arabia tagged with a tribal identification.

In the land of Uz, *there lived a man whose name was Job* – a specific person with a specific name.

This introduction has the same turn of phrase that we see in other places in scripture. Name and location.

Bible Reference
Judges 17:1

In Judges a story begins "There was a man of the hill country of Ephraim, whose name was Micah."

Bible Reference

1 Samuel 1: 1

The beginning of the story of Samuel launches with the same turn of phrase... a certain man from a certain place, with a certain name.

Comparing how other writers structure their phrasing in scripture is an indicator that this writer was not presenting this story as parable or fiction. It is possible readers would have taken this book the same way they would have read Judges or Samuel — as an account of actual events that really happened in an actual place. We know Uz was the nephew of Abraham... an actual person.

Bible Reference
Genesis 22:21

If fathers were getting prizes for naming their kids ridiculous names, then I think Abraham's brother Nahor would win hands down: Uz and Buz!

The land of Uz – refers to the land occupied by this family sub-tribe.

One of Job's friends named Elihu [is identified as a Buzite, from the tribal family of Buz – the younger brother of Uz (Job 32:2). Job also interacted with historical people groups: the Sabeans and Chaldeans (Job 1:15,17). None of this process of identifying person and place is conclusive, but it adds to the jigsaw.

Ezekiel refers to Job as a real person

Another piece of the jigsaw is that the prophet Ezekiel referred to Job as an historical person. There is a prophetic scripture in Ezekiel where the Holy spirit is making a declaration of the extent of corruption that had pervaded Israel.

Bible Reference
Ezekiel 14:14; 20

I find it incongruous that the Holy Spirit would choose two real people as examples of giants of Godly living and righteousness... and then tack on a fictional character for good measure.

The Holy Spirit is speaking of Job as a real man with incredible, outstanding integrity.

James refers to Job as real

If there is an Old Testament witness to this idea, then, are we also able find a New Testament witness as well? Yes, there is... in the letter written by James.

Bible Reference
James 5:10

James, the brother of Jesus, is writing to the early church that was facing incredible suffering... and he chooses the life of Job to inspire and encourage. He lifts Job up as an example of perseverance, patience in the face of suffering. A living breathing person... not just an imaginative, creative idea... but as someone who can inspire us in our Christian life.

Does it matter?

Does any of this matter, really, whether Job was an historical person or not? As I said before – for some people it won't matter at all... good ideas presented in various forms hold its value. For others, there is comfort in the stirring reality of real people, persevering, staying the course, and overcoming.

One writer says this when considering this question:
"We are moved to acts of bravery by the solider who earned a Purple Heart in battle; by the cancer victim who overcame all odds and survived; by the marathon runner who persevered to the finish line and then collapsed; – not by a make-believe character whose exploits of courage exist only in the realm of the imagination, a realm where there are neither the constraints of reality nor the limitations of humanity" [v]

I tend to agree. That works for me, but I'm not willing to be dogmatic about it either way. I am inclined to believe in the idea that this play was based in the reality of a historical figure whose name was Job, who lived in his ancestral home, in the Arabian region of Uz, and his story has been preserved for us, (the format of a theatrical play aside), because of the exceptional insights he gained as he wrestled with these big life questions.

Which idea do I find more comforting: that Job was a fictional character or a real person? Why?

So, let's read about this man from Uz

Bible Reading
Job 1: 1-6

There are some notable qualities and circumstances about Job that we are introduced to:

His Godly character

Job was recognised for his outstanding and honourable character:

Job is a good man; a godly man; a man who had a blameless record. He was not corrupted by immorality or dubious dealings. He honoured and worshipped God. He loved God and his ways and endeavoured to follow what he knew was right. As far as good people go, Job's character was exemplary.

His wealth and influence

Not only was Job's personal life attended to well – but Job had a community impact that was equally impressive. He had influence, presence, and authority. Not just within his own family.... but throughout the entire East.

Job also had an imposing array of stuff. This era measured wealth, not by a dollar value, but by inventory. And Job had an outstanding inventory! He was a man who was notable and noticed.

His faithful spiritual oversight

Job also was a man who took his responsibilities as the head of his family seriously. Just like Abraham, Isaac and Jacob, before the Laws of Moses were instituted, Job took on the role of Priest in his household. He took nothing for granted. He acknowledged that his children were on their own journey with God, and he prayed and interceded for them with faithful regularity.

Suffering is a series of losses

Then suddenly Job loses everything... and we will look at some of this in the next chapter. There are a series of losses that shatter his world.

His home

His home and his herds are raided and carried off by neighbouring waring nomadic tribes. Where once Job was a wealthy man... now he is bankrupt

His household members

His large family is decimated by tragedy. His sons and his daughters are tragically killed. His workforce, and household of servants suffer similar tragedy.

His health

And then finally Job's own health goes, and he suffers incredible pain with multiple health issues. There is literally very little left for Job to hang onto. His wife was still alive – but her own journey of loss leaves her bitter and resentful.

When I experience loss and suffering, is my default to blame others?

Or is it to blame God?

Or is it to blame myself?

Is there another way to make sense of difficult situations?

His social circle

Job has a few faithful remaining friends and four of them come to visit. It is their visit that becomes the basis of the dialogue in this story. The big questions they all grapple with is:
'Where is God in all this tragedy, pain and loss?'
'How can we make sense of senseless suffering?'
'What purpose is there to pain?'

Transactional or Transformational

Other wisdom literature – such as Proverbs or the Psalms, teach about the principles of sowing and reaping. Those who do right by their neighbours have the best relationships. Those who do right by their customers have the best businesses. Those who do right by those in their families have strong resilient homes. Yet here, in the story of Job, we see that these life principles do not always hold true.

I would suggest that the story of Job challenges the idea that life with God is based on a transactional model. This is the idea where, if I do good things... I will be rewarded with a good life. It is the idea that says: if I mess up... my life will be a mess.

We certainly we understand the principle of sowing and reaping – there are consequences for good choices and poor choices.

But what about those who don't make poor choices? Over and over, we have seen in the lives of people in scripture, and even those around us, where this principle is not always the case. Sometimes really good people suffer unspeakable tragedy... accidents or sickness seem to come out of nowhere. Suffering is not exclusively the domain of the morally dubious.

Suffering, pain and loss, can and does, visit anyone of us. It is in these times, that we can consider that our relationship with God is less transactional... and more transformative. A God who is with us in all circumstances. A God who can and will use these experiences to transform us, in and through all of it.

Am I more inclined to think of God as a transactional God?

What is it like to consider God engages with me in a transformative process regardless of what I am going through?

CS Lewis says this about suffering, in his book which he titled: "The Problem of Pain":

> *"We can rest contentedly in our sins and in our stupidities. and anyone who has watched gluttons*

> *shovelling down the most exquisite foods*
> *as if they did not know what they were eating,*
> *will admit that we ignore even pleasure.*
> *But pain insists on being attended to.*
> *God whispers to us in our pleasures,*
> *speaks in our conscience,*
> *but shouts in our pain:*
> *it is His megaphone to rouse a deaf world."* vi

Perhaps this is part of the answer to these big questions. God is getting our attention, and he deserves our attention, even as a response to suffering. Not to blame, or to accuse, or to demand our rights. But to listen to the message that pain might be bringing to our attention. To attend to the significance of how we are managing this painful visitor; notice what God is doing in us through these circumstances, regardless of what is happening in our world. Even in our world that might be falling apart.

So, this is what we are going to explore through the story Job. We won't go blow by blow... scene by scene... monologue by monologue. But we will look at each of the characters in this play about Job's tragedy and see what insights they can offer us as we explore our response to the issue of suffering.

Am I open to talking about these difficult realities of pain and suffering... or do I want to shut them down?

What is my reaction to the invitation to explore these ideas through reading the play of Job?

Final Thoughts...

Job is a good man, exemplary in every area of his life, yet he suffers incredible loss and tragedy... and he struggles to make sense of it all.

> *I once had a conversation with a lady in our church kitchen. She came to me and said, "Pastor, I have been very diligent with my tithing. I give an offering every week... and some-times it is hard... and I struggle to do it. But I do it because I know how important the 10% tithe is. But my problem is this... my life is not going well. I'm struggling with work. And my family relationships are stressful. And my health is not good. And my finances... as you can see, they are not blessed. If I'm tithing and doing the right thing... why isn't God coming through for me?"*

That's a good question.
If we exist in a relationship with a transactional God; if we tithe to pay-our-way... then I have no answer for this.

But I would suggest that Protestants gave up buying 'indulgences' for blessing – in this life, and in the next life, during in the Reformation. It doesn't matter what we call it, if this is our mindset... if we are stuck in a transactional model of relationship with God that is tit-for-tat, then we will expect that I do this for you... and you do that for me.

Please understand me, I believe in tithing. We tithe on our gross income all the time. We even have a spreadsheet. We do that. But tithing is not an immunisation program against life happening. It is an act of worship because we love God; we love his house; and we invest in what we love. Simple.

I made a decision when I was a pastor not to spend time in our worship service on weekly offering messages like some churches I have attended. I even had people come to me and volunteer to do this... perhaps because they thought I didn't know what they were. This conversation is one of the reasons why I chose not to do that. Somehow... along the way... after years of accumulated messages on tithes and offerings... this lady got the idea... that tithing was a formular that indebted God to make her life smooth and abundant and easy.

Tithing is not a transaction that demands God's blessing. It is a free-will offering that is a part of our love relationship with God. As we walk with God through abundant times, and times of loss, and times of suffering, God is still present with us... and he has promised never to leave us. That is the blessing!

God's transformational presence is the blessing that we have access to... through all of the things that life throws at us.

Job was a man who did everything right. Yet he is bombarded with every possible loss. And, understandably, he struggles with what is happening. That is something that I can relate to... sometimes I struggle too. As we read through this play about Job, it may help us explore some of the big questions that come from these types of experiences. Perhaps it will also offer us some insight into the common errors that come up when we are trying to answer these questions about suffering as well.

Prayer...

Father God it is a privilege to realise that you have preserved incredible stories in your scripture to help us understand what life is like. We know sometimes we don't get it, and sometimes it is very confusing and sometimes we really struggle to make sense of it all. But we thank you Father, that by your Holy Spirit, you have preserved this story about Job for us. Holy Spirit, as we explore his life and the reflections that come out of this scripture, that you would speak to us about our own personal response to pain... our own personal interaction with the reality of suffering in our lives and in the lives of those around us.

We thank you that you are a God who transforms us into people who are more aligned with your heart, whether we are living in a place of abundance, or in a season of lack and suffering. Thank you that you are with us and continue to give us strength and wisdom and courage, day by day, to do life well.

In Jesus' name, Amen.

2
The Problem of Supporting others in Suffering

Where we are...

Last week we were introduced to who Job was from the land of Uz. Job was a good man; a wealthy man; a godly man; an influential man; a family man. And suddenly, for no apparent reason his life fell apart.

I was at work one day in the office... and a woman came in, crying. This was before I had started any counselling training. Seeing people in distress is never easy.
She had just received the news that a family member had passed away. She was in shock... and we sat with her and made her a cup of tea.
Suddenly she started riffling through her bag. "I don't want to feel this! I need my medication..." she said quickly. "I need to stop feeling sad."
We helped her with her medication... but I reassured her. Feeling was important as well. Yes, it is uncomfortable... even painful... or agonising... but it tells us that what has happened is significant. It tells us that this person, and what has happened, was deeply important to us.

We can get caught in the idea that feeling is not good or not healthy, and we can spend energy on numbing-out the feeling... or trying to rush ourselves back to normal. One of the important tasks of healing... and grieving... is the 'feeling' part. As we continue into the play of Job, we see how Job engages in this feeling aspect of his grief.

We have been introduced to Job, now we are introduced to another character in this dramatic play. We are taken into the courts of Heaven.

Bible Reading
Job 1: 1-12

Introducing The Accuser

The scene that unfolds is in the kingly throne-room of heaven. The language that is used, is taken from the proceedings of an Emperor at court. A monarch, who sends out his messengers and ambassadors on important kingdom business throughout the provinces of his Empire. This king expects his subjects to give an account of what they have observed, and of the general state of the kingdom.

God is this royal sovereign. Notice there is no attempt to explain or justify God. He is who he is. The writer uses poetic imagery to help the audience wrap our mortal, time-locked, earth-bound minds around the concept of a spiritual realm that is too magnificent for us to comprehend.

And then, into this scene of addressing the business of the Empire of Earth, steps a shady character: Satan... which is literally a transliteration of the word 'Accuser'. Accuser by name. Accuser by nature.

Casting doubt on motives

Job was recognised by God for his outstanding and exemplary character, and immediately the Accuser steps forward with a *'but'*.
"But, of course, Job is doing well..."
"But, of course, he is going to worship a God who lines his pockets
He is only looking out for number one...
He is not as honourable as you make him out to be."

The Accuser is the master of casting doubt on our motives... Some of my most painful experiences have been accusations made of dubious motives, when my intentions have been sincere and honourable.
Yet the accuser doesn't hold back
He accuses Job of stacking his deck and lining his pockets.

He accuses God of pampering his subjects, and buying his worshippers with bribery, corruption and payouts.

Why is there suffering?

Now we are confronted with one of the great problems when we are considering suffering. Why is there suffering at all?
I am brought back to the great story of creation.

Bible Readings
Genesis 1:1-31.
Genesis 3:1-7

Some theologies labour the idea of the 'original sin of man'. Humanity is seen as locked in this hopeless battle against the depraved, corrupted and evil nature of sin. And yes... this is true... sin is a reality, but this is not the way God originally designed life. I think even the term "Original Sin", sounds like *this* was the beginning... the starting point. But that is not the case. God's plan was not for suffering and pain, evil and hurt... his plan was for love, and communion, and purpose, and fulfilment. *This* is the starting point the human story.

It was sin – the independence of our nature that retreats away from God, that corrupted this perfectly loving plan. By focussing on "original sin", we do find an explanation for corruption, and the pain, and the suffering, but *that* focus draws our attention away from the beautiful *original* perfect plan of creation, almost until it becomes unrecognisable. It blurs God's dogged and persistent and relentless pursuit of redeeming his good, beautiful creation.

So where is God... God who is shown to us in scripture as a loving parent, a Good Father, the grand Creator of majestic vistas? How does

God fit into this picture of suffering? Or perhaps a better question is: How does our suffering fit into the picture of God's creation?

Trying to source a 'why' of suffering requires discernment. Suffering comes from many sources:
It might be the consequences of our own choices.

I broke a coffee jar, and as I tried to pick up the shards of glass, I stabbed my finger. I chose to put my hand there. Quite intentionally. I didn't mean to be cut by picking up broken glass, but it was a choice that hurt me.

It might be the consequences of other people's choices.

Part of my story is that a person chose to drive under the influence of alcohol and drugs and then was involved in a motor vehicle collision with my parents. That was a choice that caused a great deal of pain to our family.

It might be the consequences of a broken and fallen world, waiting to be redeemed.

When we lived in North Queensland, we were in direct line of a Category-4 Cyclone as it made landfall across the coast. It was an event that caused a lot of suffering and impacted us personally. Weather events, cyclones, floods, bushfires, droughts, viruses, pandemics...
No one person holds the responsibility for these events, but things happen because we live in a world that is imperfect, and these things impact us.

Another factor might be a spiritual assignment against the people of God spearheaded by Satan... the Accuser

There have been times when I have physically felt the presence of evil. I understand clearly this was Satan's assignment against me or those I love. This is a reality of living in a spiritual world.

And there is even another option... one we don't like... the idea that, we... just... might... not... know.

Subject to the Great Sovereign

In the story of Job, we see a few of these sources of pain come to the foreground. However, what we notice in this opening dramatic scene in Job, is that regardless of the source, nothing happens without God's awareness... and nothing happens that is not filtered through God's hands.

It is helpful to remind ourselves of the sure *constants* that we do know...
We know God is good.
We know God is love.
We know God is faithful.
We know God has strong, good, loving hands who oversees all things. Even the Accuser is subject to the Great Sovereignty of God. The Accuser is restrained, even as he riles in his rebellion against God and his people.

Bible Reading
Job 1:13-22

One day... one ordinary day, when the kids are partying, and the workers are out in the paddock... suddenly everything changes. Wave after wave... tragedy follows tragedy. So, who is to blame?

The Sabeans

The Sabeans swoop in and take off with Job's impressive inventory. *"Five hundred yoke of oxen and five hundred donkeys,"* all gone at the hand of a tribal raid. Workers were massacred. The source of the suffering here, is at the hand of a Sabean tribal chieftain's decisions... someone else's choice.

Freak events

A lightning storm, a freak event that cannot be accounted for, decimated Job's sheep herds. His flock of seven thousand sheep – all gone in one freak event.

Some Bible versions say this event was the "fire of God that fell from heaven". This sounds like the writer is blaming God for causing this event, but this language is considered to be a literary device... a description for a really big storm. We might say that was *one mother of a storm*... and we are not actually blaming our mother for the rain. This was that type of *Fire-of-God* storm event.

The source of the suffering here, is living in a broken and fallen world, waiting to be redeemed.

The Chaldeans

Then in come the Chaldeans. In these ancient times, the Chaldeans were the Cushite tribal people of plains of Arabia... before they became the academics of Babylonia. Three raiding parties take off with Job's camels... a sign of his wealth and prestige.

The source of the suffering here, is at the hand of a Chaldean lord... someone else's choice.

Wave after wave... the impressive inventory that is given as we are introduced to Job, is killed, destroyed or taken away. All of it decimated, like items being crossed off on a stock-take. All gone.

Natural Disasters

And then it gets even more personal. Job's family is hit by a storm... literally and figuratively. All of his children... his large and prosperous family... tragically taken. The source of the suffering here, is the outcome of living in a broken and fallen world, waiting to be redeemed.

Wave after wave... Job could barely catch his breath... and yet Job does not blame God. He sees that the choices of tribal heads, or the events of the natural world are not God's fault. In a humble, heart-wrenching example of worship... in his grief... he throws himself into the arms of God.

Bible Reference
Job 1:20-22

"I had nothing when I started this life," he says. "I was born naked... I will die naked. God – you owe me nothing... but I will praise you while I have breath." He holds onto his knowledge that God is good.

God is not to blame! He would not charge God with wrongdoing! That is an example to take away.

And if Job's story ended here... that would be inspiration enough. But wait... there is more.

Bible Reading
Job 2:1-13

When suffering gets personal - Skin for skin

The scene cuts back into the courts of Heaven, and we are given a bird's eye view of behind-the-scenes of Job's drama. This gives us insight into the spiritual reality of our very temporal world. The writer acknowledges that there is a spiritual dimension to everything that happens on Earth.

It was not just the Sabeans and the Chaldeans who were destroying Job's life. It was not just the freaky weather events or natural disasters that decimated his livelihood and home. But there is an Accuser who desires our destruction that underpins all that is happening here.

Notice that *God* is not testing or trying to prove Job's love... this is the *agenda* of the Accuser. Jesus acknowledges the same reality:

Bible Reference
John 10:10.

Am I inclined to focus my attention on the thief who steals and destroys... or on Jesus who offers me his life affirming presence and who will never leave me?

The Accuser is a thief. His *only* agenda is to take what is not his, kill what is alive, and to destroy what is good. But notice Jesus doesn't just labour the destruction from the thief. He acknowledges it... yes... but the balance of *that* reality, is that God is the other more powerful reality... the stronger reality. He is the one who desires our wellbeing. Not just getting by, but a full life... a life that does not just survive the suffering but lives in God's fullness.

So again, back in the courts of Heaven, the Accuser suggests Job is only looking out for number one. "Of course, he will be faithful... as long as he is okay..." Satan says. We witness suffering every day... out there, but what if it gets really personal? What if it comes in close... impacts our self – to our very core?

The Accuser wants more proof. As if, taking all his stuff, and all his household, and all family, was not evidence enough of Job's integrity... now his circumstances get very personal. His physical health crashes. Yet even in this, God maintains a boundary: Job will get through this and he will survive.

What happens when I consider the idea that nothing happens without being filtered through the strong hands of God?

Do I think of God as the one who is testing me?

What changes as I notice the Accuser demands evidence and proof, whereas God loves unconditionally?

Have I ever taken on the role of the Accuser?

Sat in Ashes

There is something profoundly pathetic... in the sense of overwhelming pathos, as we witness the anguish of Job, sitting in ashes... in deep mourning. The sores covering his body represent the pain inflicted on his soul. The ashes that he sits in represents his life has been burnt to the ground. The pottery shard that he uses to scratch the unrelenting itching and irritation of his skin, represents the brokenness of his circumstances, the mutilation that offers the only slither of comfort in this moment.

These mourning rituals give voice to the unspeakable horror of what he is experiencing. There are no words

'Sitting Shiva'

Job's friends come to visit and are shocked by how this great man of the East, is now barely recognisable. They come to be with him by 'Sitting Shiva'. Shiva is derived from the word *'sheva'*, which means seven, signifying seven days of deep mourning. 'Sitting Shiva' is the Jewish mourning ritual of silently being present with someone in mourning for seven days. It is a grieving ritual that Jews still practice in Judaism. It gives space and time to the *feeling* phase of grief... and it starts the journey of healing.

How comfortable am I with feeling?

There are rules around 'Sitting Shiva' [vii], and how to be present with someone as they grieve their loss, in the most compassionate and respectful ways. They will bring food, so the grieving person does not have to worry about normal routines of hospitality. They will go bare foot and will not attend to their normal appearance and grooming. They sit low benches, or on the floor, or ground... as a symbol of the sadness, and depth of their friend's pain. There is no expectation to say anything. In fact, the opposite is true... the expectation is to be quiet, and to hold silence. They listen to what the person says... but will not speak, unless spoken to first.

How comfortable am I with silence?

Job's friends didn't say a word for this whole week of 'Sitting Shiva'. They are silent the whole time. That means Job had not spoken to them... not a word. And in turn, they respect the traditions... and his pain. *They saw how great his suffering was...*

It is hard to know how to support someone who is suffering. Our culture is very focused on fixing things. So how do we support someone in a situation that cannot be fixed? So many people do not know what to say at times like this... but they are also not comfortable with silence, so the temptation is to say anything just to fill in the gap.

> Jean Cameron was a Scottish Jacobite. The Jacobite's were the supporters of the Stuart dynasty and fought to restore them to the British throne. The name 'Jacobite' is derived from the Latin for James, Jacobus. This famous quote of Jean Cameron holds a lot of wisdom that still holds today:
> "Honest listening is one of the best medicines we can offer the bereaved..."
> (Jean Cameron – 1698-1773)

It *is* possible to honestly listen to someone's silence. This is what Job's friends were doing... during this week of 'Sitting Shiva'. There was nothing Job's friends could do or say that would make this better. So, they Sat Shiva... and were supportive, just by being present, allowing Job and themselves... to feel the *feelings* of his tragedy.

What is my reaction to the idea of Sitting Shiva with someone? Do I know someone who needs support through their experience of suffering?

Job's friends were able... not only to hold their opinions and hold the emotion... but they were also able to hold the silence. That is a beautiful gift to offer someone who needs comfort.

Final thoughts...

Job experiences unspeakable loss and tragedy in every area of his life.

As I share about this idea of Sitting Shiva that is quite foreign in our culture, I have had a number of people come to me, reflecting on times when someone had offered their presence as a gift in their grief, or where they were able to offer that to someone, they knew who had suffered great loss.

My father was telling me of a minister who went to visit a family who had suffered a great loss in their family. These people were not sympathetic to church or a life of faith, yet after his visit they were softer in their interactions. Someone asked them what wisdom this minister had offered during their loss that had made such a difference. The answer was, "He said nothing. He just sat and cried with us."
That was so comforting and was remembered as a kindness, that became part of the healing for this family, during that acute period of grieving.

This minister was Sitting Shiva. In our culture, we don't give it a formal name. It isn't a process that has traditions or defined parameters, but intuitively, this man knew what we have described for us in our Scripture. He knew a compassionate response to suffering was being present. What a beautiful gift.

We can offer support to someone in practical ways, that is a blessing. But sometimes, sitting silently with others through times of loss, and suffering, and grief that goes with that... is significant as well.

Job was bombarded with every possible loss. And yet he doesn't accuse God. Job offers God his worship; he spends time feeling the pain of his feelings; and starts the process of working through all that has happened.

Prayer...

Father, we acknowledge that the subject of suffering is very uncomfortable, but it is such a reality in our lives. We see it around us all the time in our world. Holy Spirit, we thank you that through this story of Job you have given us some insight into how we can respond to suffering. Suffering, that we experience ourselves... that we can be people that your character of Goodness, Faithfulness, and Love are constants. Help us to remember Job's inspirational example that we would not accuse you like Satan, but we would worship you. As we bear witness to suffering in other people's lives, may we more attuned to what they are going through, and offer them the gift of being present... being with them in that place with kindness and compassion. In Jesus name, Amen.

3

The Problem of a Legal Lens

Where we are...

We have seen Job was subject to multiple overwhelming tragedies. Wave after wave. And four friends came to visit him. They 'Sit Shiva' with him for a week... silently respecting his pain; being present in this ritual of deep mourning. And after that week of Sitting Shiva, Job finally speaks.

Bible Reading
Job 3:1-4; 24-26

Darkness & Despair

Job tells it like it is... and all he sees is darkness and despair. What we hear is a very honest groan coming from the pit of Job's belly. Darkness surrounds him. Where there had been light, and purpose and joy... now nothing makes sense. It is dark and oppressive.

Job wished he had never been born. It would have been *better* if he had never been born. The intensity of what he experienced was beyond his ability to manage. His life was a burden too heavy to carry.

There was a season in our lives when we were hit with wave after wave of multiple issues. My husband went for a routine medical check to renew his truck licence, and unexpectedly, the results came back with a high PSA reading. That meant he was sent for a biopsy of his prostrate. Although that result came back negative; his specialist wanted to repeat the biopsy; which showed chronic inflammation and infection which enlarged prostate. He had surgery to reduce that called a TURP. We were told he might need another in 10-15 years. We thought that concluded the matter – at least for that amount of time.

He came to me one day saying he had blood in his urine. My nurses' brain went "bing"... so we went back to the urologist to have more investigations... that showed bladder cancer. There was an extensive course of Chemotherapy – weekly visits travelling to the larger hospital and health wise he a good result. A routine biopsy diagnosed a second type of bladder cancer. More Chemotherapy – more weekly visits to travelling to the larger centre. That treatment had an adverse reaction and caused serious inflammation of the prostate, which had to be stopped. That treatment is now contraindicated. Another biopsy diagnosed suspicious precancerous cells of a third type of bladder cancer... and he has ongoing monitoring of this.

Then a scan revealed a mysterious "collection". Three experienced specialists in Brisbane consulted and no one could say for sure what it was. Surgery found it to be an abscess sitting behind the prostate that was the outcome of a rupture in the bowel wall. A random thing not related to anything else.

Another biopsy found a growth where the surgeon was unsure whether it was bladder or prostate – that was removed. Not bladder but prostate. Another TURP within was conducted within five years, because the prostate had grown to be larger than the original size before the original TURP.

Factor in other elements in our life... such as long periods of unemployment; the expense of medical specialists; episodes of anxiety from workplace bullying; my own experience of burnout and anxiety; studying deadlines; my health issues with episodes of severe chest pains that resulting in multiple hospitalisations, when investigations were not getting a clear diagnosis.

Wave after wave... and honestly, at times, it felt overwhelming.

And as I think of that time... it reminds me so much of what we have been considering in the drama of Job's life: wave after wave.

Bible Reference
Job 3:26

Is Job's deep experience of "no peace, no quietness; no rest, only turmoil" something that you have ever experienced?

Dreadful honesty

This is Job's life and these cries, are cries of his heart expressed with dreadful honesty. He is saying it – just how he is experiencing it. He isn't pretending that he understands. He isn't using platitudes to skim over the surface. He is right in the middle of this in all of its raw horror.

And the question that comes to mind... is that okay?

Is it okay for a Christian or a Godly person to feel like this?

I admire Job's authentic honesty. He is not putting on a politically correct face. He is not pretending it doesn't hurt, when it really, really does. He is not trying to protect God or accuse God. I think he is just trying to figure it out... so he can start putting back the pieces of his life.

I am going to suggest... that healing and recovery from trauma... even on the scale of Job's experience, requires that level a dreadful honesty... to move through it. What we experience internally, in our emotions is not a moral zone. In other words, what we *feel* is not right or wrong. Our emotions are not sin... or sinful. *They* are not the problem. They are but a *messenger* to inform us more about our world and what is going on. How we process and act on those feelings will determine whether we move closer to God... or further away from him.

In fact, I would suggest that if Job sat up with a smile after a week and said, "Well, how about that Mate? That was a bit rough, but I'm going to build a bridge and get over it. It's time to move on." I doubt he would feel as real, or we would feel as connected, or hold this story with as great respect as we do.

Daring to wrestle

Job was daring to wrestle with the hard emotions, and the hard questions that they evoked. I have noticed that there is a tendency in our culture to want to quickly move on to the fixing, and the solving, and the action plans. Last week we spoke about the feeling phase. There is an important place for adjusting our lives to the lost and pain, but first... feel the feelings, and then reflect and explore and understand what that means.

And this is what Job has been doing. Now he moves into the processing phase, and his four friends try to help him make sense and find meaning in this confusing and confronting pain.
As Job dares to wrestle with what has gone down, he boldly explores his faith, and his doubts, and his confusion. His four friends travel through this maze with him, and they start to present the ways that they have tried to make sense of all of this.

I encourage you to go back and read the soliloquies that have been written for each of the characters who are Job's friends, because I think that will colour in the lines that we are just sketching out in these reflections.

Introducing Eliphaz

In Chapter 4, Eliphaz the Temanite is introduced, as one of Job's friends. Teman was from the family of Esau – Jacob's twin brother. Eliphaz is identified as belonging to this family clan: a Temanite Eliphaz has a profound respect for God, and a reverent regard for God's divine majesty.

Leads the discussion

Eliphaz takes centre stage now that Job has broken the silence after the period of Sitting Shiva. Of Job's four friends, Eliphaz leads the deliberations and has the most to say. He has three lengthy monologues found in Chapters 4;5;15; & 22. It is almost like he takes the stand in a court room drama, and he rigorously defends God's honour with long and wordy speeches.

Looks through a legal lens

As we listen to what Eliphaz has to say, it becomes evident that he has a very specific lens that he is looking through. It is what I will call a 'legal lens'. It is a lens we are familiar with. It is the idea that God is a judge... a magistrate with a gavel. God rewards the innocent; God punishes the wicked.

Am I inclined to think of God as a judge in a courtroom? What brings me to make this my dominant picture of God?

Listen to how Eliphaz speaks to Job...

Bible Readings...
Job 4:5-8

Job 5:8-11
Job 22:5-13

Sowing & Reaping

Eliphaz talks a lot about the principle of sowing and reaping: Sow evil; Reap trouble. If there is one caution that the book of Job reinforces to me, it is about plucking verses out of the middle of a text and using them out of context. There are plenty of things that appear good and sound and right in this verbal processing and exploration of Job's circumstances. Much of this dialogue forms the basis of their arguments. But what all of Job's visitors, come up with at the end, is something that has deviated from the truth so far that it becomes a lie of the accuser. Where they end up... is the exact opposite of where they wanted to be. They have played into the hand of the Accuser and are doing his work for him.

If we read through Eliphaz three soliloquies, there is a progression of thought throughout Eliphaz' responses:
It starts with the principle of sowing and reaping.
It is reinforced by the principle of innocence and guilt.
It adds in the idea that God is a judge, perfectly just.
Since God can't make mistakes, your circumstances must be punishment for unconfessed or unrecognised sin.

God is good...

Eliphaz says things like: God is good. God saves the needy. God is just. God defends the vulnerable from the powerful. God is powerful, high and majestic. God's wisdom is sure. His judgements can be relied on.

You are bad...

Then Eliphaz extends this idea that God is good... because as he looks around at all the things that has happened to Job, there is no way he can say any of what has happened to Job is good! Not at all! Not in any shape or form. So, the logical conclusion that Eliphaz comes up with is: Since God is good what has happened cannot not be from God, so therefore... *you* are bad.

Yes Job, God is evidently punishing you, out of his justice. Therefore, you are bad. You are to blame. You have obviously sowed evil to reap trouble. You have obviously sinned: sneaky, subversive, sly sins... and now you are found out. God is a pure and holy judge who strictly follows the principles of sowing and reaping. He rewards the innocent and punishes the wicked.

The problem of a legal lens

Can you see how distorted his thinking has become? Eliphaz has deviated so far west, that he is no-where near where he intended to land. Back and forth, Job defends his innocence! He declares that he has not done anything to offend God

Actually, Job says... I know plenty of bad people who prosper. And I know good people who don't. Job himself maintains that he has done all the right things to the best of his knowledge. This is his great struggle. Because what Eliphas says does not make sense to him.

If what Eliphaz says is true, and Job's harsh circumstances are a judgement from God, and Job knows he has done nothing to deserve this, *this* would mean the justice of God has just gone belly up. This would mean Eliphas has arrived at the unthinkable conclusion is that goodness of God is compromised. This is the problem of a legal lens.

In what ways have I taken on Eliphaz's thinking?

Consider God's Compassion and Mercy

I would say that all those characteristics that Eliphaz identified about God *are* a facetted part of God's majestic being. *But* (and it is a big but!) they are only true if they are placed in the context of God of love and compassion.

If we take the characteristic of God's justice, for example... and if we remove it away from God's love and compassion, then God becomes a judge who is vindictive and mean and punitive. The smallest offense becomes a matter of law, not covered by grace and mercy.

But that is not who God is! We can say this categorically because we are told Jesus is the full revelation and manifestation of God the Father as part of the Trinity of God.

Jesus is God incarnate. Jesus... fully God – fully human. God cannot deny himself. God the Father cannot be one way, and Jesus the son be another way... and the Holy Spirt comes to act as some sort of mediator between the two. No! God the Father, God the Son and God the Holy Spirit, love, and act, and move, and work, in perfect unity. Always. Without exception. They continuously have... from before the foundations of the world.

Bible Reference
Colossians 2:8,9

Jesus is the Christ, Messiah... the one in which all the fullness of the triune God lives in bodily form. If our theology becomes anything less, that representation of God becomes false, and precarious, even deceptive... and actually moves across into blasphemy.

This is the trap that Eliphaz fell into... hook, line and sinker. Yes, God is good... but he is also love. So just because someone is suffering, it doesn't mean that is because they messed up, and they are being punished by God who stands as a judge, banging a gavel at them.

What happens to the picture of the judge when I consider that Jesus substitutes a different picture of God...one who is a loving father?

Jesus spoke about this to some people in Jerusalem who witnessed some terrible things that were happening in their city at that time.

Bible Reading
Luke 13: 1-5

Jesus was very adamant that the atrocities that Pilate had committed, and the tragedy of those caught in the collapsed tower
was not evidence they were worse sinners than the rest of the Jews living in the city at that time. God was not sitting in judgement and punishing them over the other citizens. No... Not at all!

But Jesus also follows that observation with a sober reminder that we all have a responsibility to live aligned with God... to turn to him... to keep coming back to his arms. Just because those he was talking with had not been murdered, or had escaped the terrible tragedy of the tower, this was not evidence of their vindication or innocence before God either.

This is because the figure of God as a courtroom judge is less accurate than the picture of God as a Father who desires his children to turn back to him. A life without God... that is its own eternal death.

Who do I know who needs the reassurance that God loves them, and is not judging them by sending pain and suffering?

How could I communicate this?

Baxter says this about looking at the gospel through a legal lens like Eliphaz:

"The framing of the gospel itself, in the legal model, teaches us that there is a side of God that does not like us at all, a side that would just as soon have us miserable and broken and enslaved to darkness...
The amazing truth is that this Triune God, in staggering and lavish love, determined to open the circle and share the Trinitarian life with others.
There is no other God, no other will of God, no second plan, no hidden agenda for human beings.
From the beginning, God is Father, Son and Spirit, this God has determined not to exist without us." [viii]

This legal lens, of Job's friend Eliphaz, distorted this truth about God. Yes, God is good, and he is great, but the larger truth is about his staggering and lavish love. Over and over, Jesus changes the language of how he talks about God: From Judge... to Father; from the courtroom... to family, parents and children; from a legal process... to the love covenant of marriage.

Final thoughts...

Job starts to process the terrible things that have happened to him... but his friend Eliphaz is looking through a legal lens.

I remember sharing some of the circumstances that I mentioned earlier with some very experienced pastors. Wave, after wave, after wave. I shared how that season was hard... discouraging... painful. And the tone of the response to sharing this personal journey was...
"Well perhaps you were not praying enough... or perhaps you weren't reading your bible enough... or perhaps if you had done more... you would have been able to see victory."
I remember speaking up and putting pause on that line of thinking straight away. No... actually my devotional and prayer life was strong... I was praying, and fasting, and worshiping as part of my normal life. That part of my life needed to be strong! I had done nothing 'wrong'. I was ticking boxes... if the boxes needed to be ticked. This wasn't happening because I was a poor Christian making poor choices. It wasn't an outcome of sowing sloth, or dallying with evil, or making compromising choices.
This was just happening!

As I think of that interaction... it reminds me so much of what we have considered today. This is Eliphaz thinking! Even in our experience of God's grace; even as mature Christians, with our own personal encounter with God's love and mercy; somehow, we can still come up with the idea that God is judging us. Or that we don't measure up. Or that we are sowing what we are reaping, and we are to blame. That somehow our Christian experience is a legal process rather than a love process.

How much more accurate it is to consider the idea that God is our *loving parent*... who is with us in all of our pain, and the heartache... and he desires us to be family with him. Together.

Prayer...

Father God, we acknowledge that some of the things we go through, and the things we witness other people go through are so hard. It is our default sometimes to clutch at straws to provide some sort of explanation for what is happening. But Father, forgive for the times when we have engaged in Eliphaz thinking, and we have set the blame on the other person. Perhaps we have even set the blame on you as a judge. Father, forgive us. We want to be people with the mind of Christ and who thinks like Jesus, that honours the truth of who you are. Yes, you are mighty, and yes you are majestic, but you also embrace us as family. You desire good for us. Thank you that you are with us through all of the things we experience, and you are with us even when we feel weak.
In Jesus name, Amen.

4
The Problem of Projecting

Where we are...

We have considered the arguments of Job's friend Eliphaz as he looked through a legal lens to try and explain why Job was experiencing multiple overwhelming tragedies. Now we look at the next friend of Job and how he interprets Job's situation.

Introducing Bildab from the Shuhites

Like his friends, Bildab is given a specific epitaph that points to the family and place he is from: He is a Shuhite. Shuah was one of the sons of Abraham, that he had when he married Ketura, after Sarah died, so Shuah was a half-brother to Isaac.

Culturally - a powerful people

There is some who think that Shuah's tribe occupied the western region of Chaldea, bordering Arabia, along the Euphrates River. There have been found Assyrian inscriptions in those locations referring to the Tsahi [pronounced: za-hee] people. They were recognised as "a powerful people". It is possible these Tsahi people were Shuhites. If that is the case, then Bildab was part of this ancient fierce and powerful culture. In this culture, power equates to winning, dominating, exerting authority... most likely through ferocity and violence.

Perspective of Power & Punishment

As I read through Bildab's speeches, I notice that Bildab is big on the idea of punishment. If he comes from a powerful people who use force to maintain order in their culture, then it it follows that his perspective of God, who is the most powerful of all, is seen by him as a God who uses force and punishes to maintain his power and authority.

Can you think of an example of something you grew up believing was a biblical truth, only to discover it was a personal or cultural interpretation?

Let's read some excerpts from Bildab's speeches...

Bible Reading:
Job 8:1-6
Job 18:2-5; 18-21
Job 25:2-6

Power and Punishment

Bildab, like Eliphaz, has a strong sense of God's magnificent authority. "Remember," he declares, "God is mighty!" He reminds Job that God is mysterious and omniscient. He is the one who has dominion and power. God is big and majestic and awesome.

If you repent; God will relent

But rather than being encouraging and uplifting, I find Bildab's speeches dark and condemning. God might be light, and make the sun rise, but there is the parallel idea that anything that is not equally majestic, is an outcome of God's condemnation and punishment. Bildab also falls deeply into the blame-game.

Laying the blame increased Job's suffering, rather than alleviating it. Notice how Bildab speaks rather sarcastically at times. "You're not taking what I am saying seriously!". Using a metaphor from the cattle-herders, he says, "You think I am a dumb old cow!" Ultimately, Bildab believes we are all just dirty rotten sinners: worms and maggots. He insists Job is in denial and he needs to repent.

Bildab believes that God is intent on harm, in the name of justice. But... if we play our cards right... God will relent... change his mind... and will be converted to the idea of lifting his harsh resolve to punish us. Do you see the error? God doesn't need to change his mind about us because his mind is always for us... not against us. God doesn't need to be soothed or placated. That is the mindset of heathen religions not the truth of who Jehovah God is.

Rendering Culture as Spiritual truth

Yet the idea of punishment persists throughout Bildab's speeches. He has taken an idea and experience that is cultural and made it a spiritual truth, a moral absolute. Can you see how the projection of his experiences colours his argument?

He starts with the idea that God is powerful. Then believes that the balance of power will therefore always be with those God holds in favour. Then he pursues the idea that a powerful God punishes the sinful with penalties according to their wrongdoing. But this projection of God is a cultural one, not a spiritual truth at all.

His people were a people of violence, payback and punishment. He is looking through a cultural lens, of power, and authority, and punishment... and then projects an image of God that is not an accurate portrayal of who God is and how he interacts with his people. He doesn't consider God's mercy and loving kindness at all in his deliberations.

Bible Reference
Deuteronomy 4:31

When might I filter my understanding of God through my cultural lens?

At one point in our parenting journey, we participated in a Christian bible-based parenting program. I thought that was a good idea. But as we progressed through the material, I found much of what they were teaching, was translating parenting through a cultural lens, and that would work... if I belonged to that particular culture.
But... I don't.
I did not think my sons were being disrespectful because I didn't send them to church every Sunday in a 3-piece suit. We lived in tropical Queensland. That didn't work for me... or them.
My husband does not think I am being disrespectful, because I stand up and speak in front of people, rather than staying silent and seated. This exercise almost became ludicrous in the end, because their lens was so removed from the realities of our cultural expressions, but it was being taught as Truth with a capital T.
What that experience did make clear for me, is that many of our Church experiences can be cultural, rather than spiritual. And again, that is okay... as long as we recognise them as such.
The problem comes when we translate culture and preference, as the directives from the Holy Spirit... and the start to believe that there is no other way to do church. If we become dogmatic in our assertions that we know the

right way to understand God, we are misrepresenting God and his family. There can be difference and still be part of his big, wonderful, diverse family

What sort of things do I take as non-negotiable that may actually fall into this cultural space?

Final thoughts...

Job's friends continue the process of trying to convert Job to their understanding of his situation. And as we will see... there are matters of the heart that Job is unwilling to compromise on.

Prayer:

Father God, we appreciate that you have place each one of us in unique cultural situations... even in our families, or nationalities. Help us to distinguish between what are non-negotiable faith tenets and what is cultural norms and preferences. Help us to be mindful of what other people see and understand as respectful, but most of all, look first to you and your word about how we choose to conduct ourselves.

5
The Problem of Not Listening

Where we are...

Eliphaz and Bildab have taken the stage to explore why Job was experiencing suffering and pain. But their stance of legalising and projecting cultural understandings of God does not address the issues of Job's suffering. In fact, it exacerbates it. Now we are introduced to Job's next friend Zophar and he also expounds his understanding of Job's situation.

Introducing Zophar of unknown lineage

We are told Job's third friend... Zophar was from the Naamathites. I could not find any information about who the Naamathites were. It is not clear where these people lived, and there are no other references to his tribal group, outside the book of Job, that I could find.

We have two soliloquies from Zophar – in Chapters 11 and 20.

Bible Reading:
Job 11:1-6;14-17
Job 20: 1-8

Has not listened

What we do know about Zophar is that has not listened to the anguish of Job. He may have heard his argument... his words, but he has not heard his heart... or his pain. He does not understand, or 'get' what it was like for Job to go through the tragedy that he has experienced.

Zophar is patronising in his talk

He becomes vehement in his efforts to covert Job to his thinking, and it ends up looking something like this: "I have God figured out... and... I have *your* problems figured out. "There is an arrogance in Zophar's speeches that leaps off the page in bold print. There is no pause; there is no acknowledgement of margin. This is just absolutely the way that it is. His black-and-white thinking is very condescending and patronising. He believes Job needs the enlightenment of his truth! And he makes no apologies that he is the bearer of this truth. There is no allowance that he might be the one who needs to hear a different perspective.

Job responds

Finally, Job has his turn to speak. And he says things that now start to sound equally frustrated and sarcastic as his friends

Bible Reading:
Job 19:2-5
Job 26:2-4
Job 27:3-6

Condemnation adds to pain

We notice that the judgements of his friend were adding to his pain, not alleviating his suffering. We notice that the blame game was heaping additional emotional pain, on his already devastated life. The way they saw life and interpreted his situation was full of condemnation, and did nothing to help him understand or resolve his dilemmas.

The rhetoric is confusing

It was not only 'not helpful', but it was confusing. Job was seeking clarity... not more murky arguments.

Why does it not comfort Job to be told over and over that God is good?

Job actually already knew this. This was part of his belief system. Even with what was going on Job held onto the conviction that God was above reproach. But it was not helping Job to be told over and over that God's ways are perfect. In his responses, he has acknowledged this. We can see Job already had his own understanding of God, but how that looked right now... beside the graves of his family, scratching his weeping sores in piles of ashes... it was dark and confusing. And what was being said, added to his pain... not alleviated it.

Job will not confess, just to satisfy

What we do notice is that Job refuses to say what his friends want him to say. He won't confess to guilt just to satisfy them... or even to get them off his back. He continues to want to stay true to what he does know... even in the midst of so much that he doesn't know.

I know my redeemer lives!

And then, right in the middle of all of this tossing backwards and forwards of doubt, arguments and reflections, there is one statement that Job says, which becomes an anchor point for him:

Bible Reading:
Job 19:25

"I know!" he declares. "I know that my redeemer lives, and that in the end he will stand on the earth. I know that I will see this with my own eyes!"

I did a little experiment to see if something I had observed had merit. Speech after speech... as Job explores his faith and his doubt, his pain and his trouble... right in the middle of all this he makes this profound prophetic declaration. Ten speeches one side, and ten speeches the other side... This statement stands out like a lighthouse in amongst all his trouble!

"I know my redeemer lives!"

Job | Eliphaz | Job | Bildad | Job | Zophar | Job | Eliphaz | Job | Bildad | Job: "I know my redeemer lives!" | Zophar | Job | Eliphaz | Job | Bildad | Job | Elihu | Job | God | Job

In the midst all of the things that Job didn't know... this is what he did know! It shines like a beacon in the middle of all this darkness.
"I know that my redeemer lives!"
"I will see God with my own eyes..."
"I will... me... not someone else"
"How I long for that!"

This is the hope that secures Job in all of his suffering. In all of his confusion. In all of the judgment, and blame, and heartache, and physical torment. This was the one sure thing that he knows. This becomes the anchor around which all of the other shifting ideas and unstable arguments that are going on, are held.

Do I have one central conviction that is the anchor for my life...

This observation is very Hebrew in its structure. It is called "reverse concentric symmetry". It is a literary device where one central idea is anchored from which other ideas are mirrored and pivots around that main idea. I thought this was remarkable. What a wonderful idea for us to take hold of when things are dark and confusing. To find our anchor point that becomes a solid hold to place our hope.

The writer of Hebrews declared his anchor point was the priesthood of Jesus:

Bible reference:
Hebrews 6:18-20

God's character is unchangeable and trustworthy, and our secure hope is that Jesus is our Christ, how High Priest who intercedes for us.

A Caution from Job's friends

Looking over Job's first three friends' and their advice; the way that they talk, I think they offer an example of some common mistakes that can be made. It is worth noting them so we can be mindful not to fall into the same traps. When I think about the story of Job, I reckon that his friends did quite well... until they opened their mouths!

That is perhaps the first caution... be sensitive of what we say. It is worthwhile to acknowledge that we can start in the right place and end up at the wrong destination, if we don't be aware of our transitions.

Just because we understand one truth, doesn't automatically mean the rest of our case is sound. We need to be careful how we join the dots. Mixing God's truth with our logic, or our culture, or our bias... can cause massive deviations from the reality of God's heart. Both Eliphaz and Bildab had a solid starting point; they begin by saying God is good, and majestic, and powerful... but then they join dots to bring them to land a long way from the truth of God's heart.

It is okay to acknowledge that we know this much, but after that, we are not sure. In fact, this is the better approach. It prevents making wild leaps in the dark, hoping that we arrive somewhere close.

Saying the right thing in the wrong way

Another caution is that we can say the right thing but in the wrong way, so that distorts the whole content. Even if everything that Job's friends said had been technically accurate, it has been delivered without compassion, without humility, and without modesty.

If I yell at you with a scowl and declare "God is love!", what is the message that you hear?

Compassion... the kindness of God... his sacrificial love? No – the message that is heard is loud, aggressive, and overbearing... and that is not the spirit of love. It is certainly not the Spirit of God. Although the content of what is said might be technically true, after all, 'God *is* actually love', the message becomes distorted by the way that it is delivered.

Have I ever said the right thing the wrong way, and missed the opportunity to have influence?

Zophar is an example of delivering his black and white thinking by packaging his message in a way that is patronising and arrogant/. Anything that he may have said, that could have been helpful to Job, is lost in the tone of his delivery.

Speaking to convert...

One of the great challenges of any discussion, is the temptation to hear, without listening. We might listen, but all the while be compiling a rebuttal in our head, or an argument to refute, so to have our point of view acknowledged as the correct one, becomes our driving motivation. "I am right, and I need to prove that you are wrong"

When I was on the debating team at school... we were trained to listen for the rebuttal. We spoke to prove a point; to convert the audience; to convince them of one point of view; to win the argument... whether we believed it or not. This can become a habit. It became my habit. But life is not a debate to convince, or an argument to win. Communicating is more about relationship than point-scoring. That changes when we listen (not to convert someone to our point of view), but to listen to understand the other person's perspective and experience...

Learning to Listen

To truly listen we open ourselves up to the idea of appreciating someone's perspective, their thinking, their pain, their joy. To hear –

not just the person's words, but the heart of what they are saying as well. I don't think Job's friends really understood that we can compassionately hear another's story without having the need to answer all the questions, or respond to all the doubts, or have consensus of opinion.

We can listen without needing to agree on every point. We are grown-ups now! It is okay to hold a different perspective. Consensus is not the goal, listening to understand is. We can listen without changing our convictions. We can listen without compromising our values and what is important to us.

The debate of Job's friends, and their efforts to convert Job to their thinking, by trying to get him to embrace their perspectives serves and achieves one thing in the end: it increases Job's suffering and does nothing to alleviate it.

> *Our human need...*
> *There is a quote from Ralph Nichols that says this:*
> *"The most basic of all human needs is the need to be understood and to understand. The best way to understand people is to listen to them."*
> *~Ralph Nichols~*

Recall a time when you have not been listened to. What was that like? What is different when you have been truly heard?

Final thoughts...

In all of this journey of debate by presenting arguments to build their case, Job is not understood. He is not heard. He is not listened to.

One Sunday I was sitting with a visitor at church. This was before I knew anything about counselling or really understood the power of being heard. This lady was quite frail, and she shared with me some very deep losses in her life. We sat at the back of the church while she talked, and I just started to cry with her as she shared her journey.

She became very apologetic. "I'm so sorry to upset you!" and I could feel that she was retreating because of my tears.

And I said to her... "No, I'm not distressed. But I hear what you say... and sometimes I think it is okay just to have someone who will sit and cry with us." That probably would have been one of those sacred moments that I would file away... except her daughter came up to me the next Sunday and thanked me. She told me that her mother had spoken to her when they got home. "People say they listen all the time, but usually they don't. It is rare to know that someone has really listened and heard."

That comment impacted me greatly. How many times have I kidded myself that I am listening? What I have actually been doing is trying to work out what I am going to say next; or wanting to soothe my own discomfort; or satisfy this compulsive need to fix the problem with my solutions. As I think of how that beautiful lady shared her heart with me, it reminds me so much of the power of listening... not just listening to content... but listening with our heart.

If we don't listen, we could end up being what my Mum used to call, "a Job's comforter". That was not a compliment by the way. Someone who foolishly ends up exacerbating someone's pain, when they have come to us for comfort.

How much more beautiful to know that we can be God's arms to hug, and God's ears – to not just hear words, but to listen with our heart, to another's heart.

As we meet with people, in all of their confusing pain, let's listen to their hearts first. God desires us to be people who live well and wholly, who love unconditionally, who laugh and share other's joy, and listen with our hearts. Being present with others - Together.

Prayer...

Father God it is a privilege to journey with other people, whether they be people in our family circle, social circle, work circle or church circle. You have positioned each one of us intentionally in these places. We ask Father, that as we rub shoulders with others that we would be people who hear first... listen with our hearts to what other people are really saying. Help us not be dismissive of other people's pain as they journey through all sorts of life circumstances, but that we would be available in these encounters. May they find a reflection of your heart of love towards them, through us.
In Jesus Name, Amen.

6
The Problem of Spiritualising

I wonder what you would think if I started this reflection by saying...
"What we will cover today will blow the lid off every conception you have about God. I am going to change your thinking and your life! What I will share with you will have you walking away from this book with a whole new perspective!"
First – you will probably think I've lost my mind.
Then you will probably do what I did... when I heard a '20-something' start his Sunday message with that attempt at a dynamic introduction.... I sat there and thought... "Really... in 20 minutes, you are going to unravel 40 years of my journey with God. I don't think so. Pretty sure nothing you will say is going to be that dramatic. But I can see you are going to give those claims a pretty good crack, because you seem really invested. This is going to be something!"
Well... it wasn't something... because I can't remember what was said... apart from that rather exceptional introduction... which was burnt into my brain.
It did, however, highlight, the idea that the enthusiasm of youth... can definitely come across as presumptuous, arrogant... and ignorant... if it is not tempered with a heavy dose of humility and diffidence.
In fact,... that sort of enthusiasm... whether coming from someone who is young or old, when is framed in a way that indicates "I know and you don't", would always fall into that category of presumption, arrogance and ignorance... and it is something that we are considering in this part of Job's story.

Where we are...

We've met three of Job's friends: Eliphaz, Bildab and Zophar.
Today we meet the fourth friend who had come to sit shiver with Job.

Bible Reading:
Job 32:1-10

Introducing Elihu, Son of Barakel the Buzite

Like his friends, Elihu is given a specific tag that points to which family he is from: He is the son of Barakel, the Buzite. Elihu is from the clan of Buz. Remember Uz and Buz? So Elihu, as a Buzite, was from a related clan to Job, who was from the family of Uz. In some cultures, we might say they were loosely associated as 'cousins'.

The youngest of the four friends

So, the first three friends have given up talking now. Their arguments have not convinced. Their intent to convert Job's perspective has not been accomplished. And then... almost in a final effort to justify their stance, they diagnose that Job has remained "righteous in his own eyes." That is their final verdict. "Job: you are blind; you are in denial; you have a hard-heart, and you are unwilling to repent."

"Job, we are right – and you are in the wrong! You are stubborn... and doomed."

So Eliphaz, Bildab and Zophar sit back now. They have thrown their hands up in despair and have nothing more to say. Finally.

Then the fourth friend, Elihu, who has sat silent until now... starts to speak. He is the youngest of the four friends. He begins his speech with all the language of respect and diffidence to his elders.

But as he launches into his soliloquy there is actually nothing reserved or hesitant about his manner. He quickly becomes the loudest voice. The others have failed, so it is up to him now. He has the answers that the others could not offer. He has the solutions, that the others could not source.

The master of spiritualising

As I read through Elihu's speech, I notice this arrogance of youth coming through, even though he places that very definite disclaimer right at the start. There is something else that comes through... and that is the problem of spiritualising.

Spiritualising is making everything a spiritual problem, rather than allowing for other realities to be part of our experience as well. But you might say, isn't God the source of everything, at the core of every aspect of our lives? Doesn't that make everything spiritual in nature? Paul puts it this way in his letter to the Ephesians:

Bible Reference
Ephesians 4:6

Yes, God is a part of every aspect of life – this is true: over all and *through* all... and *in* all. Even though we know that God is the source of our lives, and he is in it all, that doesn't mean that we can sweep away problems, because we give them a spiritual meaning.

Spiritualising is not attempting to recognise God's intimate presence in the very fabric of our lives, nor is it separating out and compartmentalising our lives into secular and spiritual. Spiritualising becomes a way of avoiding aspects of our lives that need attention. It is a way of taking the reality of the many facets of our experience and whitewashing it all as "spiritual".

Our lives cannot be compartmentalised, whether they are concrete events, temporal experiences, emotional, intellectual, relational, social, physical aspects of our lives. However, if everything is ascribed a spiritual overlay, spiritualising becomes an excuse, rather than a healthy, grounding reality.

When everything becomes a Spiritual problem, rather than expanding our options... it shrinks them. My role is limited to confession and repentance, and then it is up to God. I abdicate my personal responsibilities and accountabilities. It can quickly become *'Que Sera Sera'* – Whatever will be... will be. It starts to look like fatalism, or resignation, submission to fate... a fate that is in God's hands.

This is not the life Jesus talks about. He desires us to be in relationship with our Father God who is a loving parent... who walks with us through all of our life circumstances, who asks us to participate in this life, hands open, freely chosen, taking hold of the good choices available to us, as much as it depends on us.

Bible Reference
John 10:10
Matthew 29:20

Jesus talks about a full and satisfying life. He offers this as one who will never leave us or forsake... and certainly, he will not abandon us to some spiritual fate in the hand of a far off and remote God.

Let's read an excerpt from Elihu's speeches...

Bible Reading
Job 36:1-10

Spiritualising using Personal catchcries

Elihu, like the others, has a strong sense of God's exalted righteousness. But he uses these words as personal catchcries.
God is Mighty!
God is exalted!
I will ascribe justice to my Maker!
God supports the afflicted!

These things are true, but when they are used as a cover-all, they lose their power. They are phrases put out there to cover over our own discomfort with what is happening: *"I know you are going through hell but hey God is good."*

> I watched an ABC documentary which was part of a series called, "You can't ask that." On one program they interviewed some people who were significantly disfigured.
> One lady spoke about being in a shop one day when a woman walked past her and then came back to her and said, "I think you are so beautiful, and Jesus loves you."
> The lady who was being interviewed, as she was recalling this encounter, said very frankly: "That really pisses me off."
> Why would that be?
> On the surface it sounds like a kind of caring and affirming thing to say. But it was actually using a platitude as fix-it-all. It is spiritualising... and it did not consider what it was like to be that person... in her body... in her reality. And in the end, it became intensely disrespectful.

Can you give an example of spiritual catchcries, that misses the opportunity to really be present, and to love people who need to know someone cares?

Patterns of avoidance

Another problem with spiritualising is that it becomes a justification for bypassing what is really going on. We use God to detour around, or bypass the pain, and the anger, and the hurt. rather than engage with it, to navigate through it towards healing. We avoid those things, because they are painful for us to engage with them. We bypass the things that challenge our own thinking and awareness, because it is uncomfortable to look at them directly.

Elihu avoids the issue of Job's pain completely! Never once docs he say... "I see you are hurting and grieving." He uses God's name as a reason to justify skipping the horrifying reality of Job's experience.

Instead, he talks incessantly about God's creative majesty, his power and justice, his authority and magnificence. Again... these characteristics of God are real... but not outside the context of his love, his kindness, and compassion. God never avoids the reality of our experiences, in all of its ugliness. No... God actually joins with us, to be with us in those places. It is worth noting that if Elihu had even talked incessantly about God's loving compassion... that could also have been another example of spiritual bypassing if it is used to wash-over and avoid the discomfort of what is really going on.

Paths that lead away, not towards

Do you see the problem here? Compassion and empathy are God's heart, and all this talk about God's majestic nature doesn't allow Elihu to connect into how deeply God loves Job.

It skirts around it; it bypasses it.

Elihu doesn't connect into loving Job more effectively himself. It leads him away from making that investment. It doesn't allow Elihu to explore his own pain and distress of what is happening. He pushes that all underground and he doesn't allow it to surface... because after all, as he says: "God is Mighty!" That is the pat answer to everything.

Was I aware that I could use my Christianity to avoid and skim-over what is really going on?

What sort of things do I do, that might look like Elihu's spiritual bypassing?

> *Robert Masters says this:*
> *"It has been easier to frame spiritual bypassing as...*
> *spiritually advanced practice or perspective,*
> *It is epitomized by fast-food spirituality...*
> *drive-through servings of reheated wisdom..."*[ix]

Elihu's speeches is full of fast-food gems. His spiritualising shuts him down; it shuts him off from what is really going on. His friend is hurting, and what Job needs, is someone with skin on to love him. Now.

But his spiritualising leads Elihu away from that... and consequently, leads him away from God's heart.

Leans towards Spiritual Abuse

What becomes more disturbing about all this spiritualising, is that it not only prevents Elihu from dealing with his own discomfort, and Job's discomfort, but it also creates more tension and more distress. It sounds so spiritual, and so knowledgeable, and so wise... and so mature... but... it actually becomes a tool for creating more pain.

Have you ever met anyone who has a bible verse for everything... even the weather? I had someone tell me after a major Cyclone event that since we couldn't go to Third-World cultures ourselves, this was God's way of bringing me the challenges of the third world to our own back yard, just as if we were missionaries.
When I said I really wasn't excited by that idea, and I really did want the power back on so we could just flush our toilet, I got the impression she thought I was letting the side down.
Was the cyclone a spiritual event? No. It was a weather event. Could God use a weather event? Oh yes, I know that he did. Many people have shared their stories with me, so know that was absolutely the case, but right then, I needed someone who wasn't spiritualising, but willing to acknowledge that I was finding it challenging to cope with all the destruction, and the stress, and the disorientation that such an event creates.
Does it mean I didn't love Jesus because I wanted a flushing toilet?
Did I not have the faith to cope with that scale of a natural disaster without a blip? I'm going to suggest what psychologists tell us, that this type of event stretches our coping – physically, mentally and emotionally... and it is to be

expected that it is difficult to manage. We don't have to make it a spiritual problem.

Spiritualising muddies the water... and it can pile guilt and anxiety on top of existing pain. That means that spiritualising becomes another instrument of pain. It becomes a weapon that ends up hurting rather than supporting and encouraging and healing. Regardless of what one intends, in that way, spiritualizing becomes a tool in the hand of the Accuser.

Elihu is not the only one. He has fallen into the same style of speech as his three elders. He is trying to control and out-work one specific outcome. And the outcome that he wants, is not actually the same outcome that God wants to see happen...

Bible Reading
Matthew 22:36-40

What is to be the outcome or goal of our interactions?

It is moving away from the outcome God desires, but Elihu does it in the name of God anyway. When this happens, it tips into manipulation, controlling and abusive.

Using God's Name in vain

It is using the name of God to achieve something that we want: to serve our own ends. This is what it means to "Use the Lord's name in vain". This is the third commandment of the Law of Moses.

Bible Reference
Exodus 20:7

Taking the Lord's name in vain, is not just carelessly swearing or mindlessly saying "God!" or "Jesus!" That might be a form of it. Holding God's names reverently, should be done with the same respect we would exercise when we talk about the people we love and care for. But more significantly – when we use God's name... and his credibility, to get our own way and to manipulate others for our own outcomes... we are breaking the third commandment. In old fashioned terms it is like we are signing a cheque by forging God's signature, for something that God never authorised us to purchase, or said he would do. It is also abusive and controlling and it is not okay.

Have I ever falsely signed a cheque in God's name?

What was the result of that?

How could I be more honest about what God can and does deliver?

Invitation not Mandate

One way... is to take a step back and to notice what is driving the things that we are saying and doing? Another way is to offer an invitation, rather than demand a mandate. It is humbly acknowledging that we don't have God all sewn up. We are not God's gift to humanity as a revelation of His truth. That was Jesus.

We introduce others to Jesus... that's our part. The Holy Spirit does the rest. Yes, we are his children: his servants and his handmaidens... his practical hands and his feet... and our first obligation is to love. To care. To share. To teach and disciple. It is never forcing or mandating or manipulating. The invitation Jesus gives to us is to introduce others to him. Scripture says that "it is the kindness of God... that leads to repentance"

Bible Reference
Roman 2:4

I wonder what it would have been like, if Job's four friends had been a little bit kinder, and a little bit wiser, in the way they expressed their beliefs, in caring for Job and loving him in all of his distress? I suspect that would have made a huge difference to Job's experience.

Final thoughts...

Job's fourth friend, Elihu, stands-up and picks-up where the others have given-up. He continues trying to convert Job to his much superior understanding of Job's situation. And the problem of Spiritualising is a noticeable trend in Elihu's thinking.

This idea of making things a spiritual problem, when it is not primarily a spiritual problem can lead us into all sorts of errors. Every situation needs discernment and wisdom from the Holy Spirit so that we attentively addressing what is at the core that needs our attention.
Part of my story has been an experience of burnout...
I had been working bi-vocationally in a full-time job and at the same time I also held a significant volunteer role at my church, as a campus-pastor. I was effectively working two full time jobs... and it wasn't sustainable. Unlike super-heroes, I had forgotten I don't wear my underpants on the outside. That constant pressure took its toll.
I noticed that some people were quick to diagnose my situation as a spiritual problem... something about my relationship with God was flawed, for this to happen. After all – I was told, if I was doing all this for Jesus... and my heart was in the right place, these things wouldn't happen... couldn't happen.
But what was going on, wasn't a spiritual problem... it was a matter of not having the mental and physical reserves to keep up that sort of pace. I didn't have the emotional reserves to meet those expectations.
But as I engaged with professionals... balanced Christian practitioners, I saw that my relationship with God was not on the line. God still loved me. 'Unconditionally', still meant unconditionally. Yes, I had worked for a long time without taking a break. Yes, I surrounded myself with people who pushed me to do more, rather than supporting me to be accountable about sensible selfcare. I had broken the principle of taking Sabbath Rest for years and that stress accumulated and had consequences that were serious. God institutes these guidelines for our wellbeing.
Ignoring that meant my rubber-band had lost its flex. I had no bounce-back left. I can't say that I didn't know about emotional care, or mental health hygiene, but I didn't know how else to do, (what I believed), I was obligated to do. Part of the problem was that I listened to the Elihus in my life. I believed

what they said, and it coloured the way I understood God and his expectations of me.
But just because I was doing all this in the name of Jesus, this didn't make me immune to the dynamics of my mental health eroding, or my emotional wellbeing crashing. One of the healthier trends in workplaces, including church ministry, is a greater awareness of a balanced, holistic attention to all aspects of our lives... being mindful of physical care, and emotional care, and mental self-care and relationship care.
It was a relief for me to know that what I was going through... was not actually a spiritual problem... it was a mental health and emotional health issue... And I needed to address those things. This discernment gave me options to know how to source support so I could recover and heal.

I can picture many people, who I have supported over the years, who have cried with relief, when they really understood that what they were going through was not a spiritual problem. It was a problem. Can't deny that... but they were not bad Christians... and even if they had dropped the ball in some way... God is still a resource in our pain... and in our healing... not the cause of it... and he certainly doesn't abandon us to it.

How wonderful that God is in our healing! During that season of restoration, God surrounded me with supportive people who helped me go towards my pain, to look at it and address it, rather than avoiding it or bypassing it... in the name of Jesus.

It can be very easy to say, "Jesus is the answer," as a way to avoid what the question may actually look like. Whenever these professional people, who were positioned around me, if they identified that I was tempted to start spiritualising... they called me on it. They did. Gently. Always with an invitation... that when I was ready, to come back to it... to do more to care for myself emotionally and mentally, and they were there to support me to do that. I needed that sort of accountability, rather than the pressure to push further, and do more with less.

Are there areas in my life, (emotional, mental, physical, relational) where I need to show more care for myself?

What is it like to know that God is my healer, and he may use other people-with-skin-on to support me as well?

Yes, I can say that Jesus is my Healer. I am humbly aware, that some people do not come back from burnout. I know God is the reason I am able to function well now. But I also need to acknowledge that he used beautiful people, who were willing to come along side me... not with Elihu arrogance, or fast-food religious platitudes, but with authentic care and grace and patience.

They were present with me through some pretty ugly stuff. Together.

What a wonderful invitation this story has for us to be present with others in a healthier, supportive way.

Prayer:

Father God, sometimes it is really easy for us to dish up fast-food platitudes because it covers our discomfort, and it covers our own

uncertainty about what is happening, and we do want to believe that everything will be alright. Thank you, Holy Spirit that you are with us. Help us to pause and to defer to your wisdom. Give us discernment so that we know what we are dealing with. Give us sensitivity to know what to say... but perhaps more importantly, recognise what we are *not* to say. Above all, Holy Spirit, may we be people who bear your fruit of patience and kindness and care with others.
In Jesus Name, Amen.

7
The Problem of God's Sovereignty

Where we are...

So, we have come to the final act of the dramatic play of Job.

We have heard the four arguments of Eliphaz, Bildab, Zophar and Elihu. And it seems like nothing is gained, the conflict remains, no resolution is achieved.

I once needed to have a scan. The technician turned to me and said with a smile... "No problems here... everything looks really healthy. Off you go..."
I was in shock... stunned... and in gut-wrenching grief. The scan was to confirm if I had lost a pregnancy. And the only thing I could think to do was to go down and sit by the Condamine River... and watch the calm of the water... the stillness... and the brilliant blue dragonflies hovering over the water, above the surface... rising above the pain in some way.
I had a very real sense as I sat there... that God was sitting with me in this storm... and he had created a still place for me. He was present with me in this pain.
This idea of finding a still place in the storm is what we are going to look at today as we conclude our reflections around the story of Job.

The fifth person sitting shiva

Then there is a surprising great reveal, as the finale builds. We meet the fifth friend who had come to sit shiver with Job. Yes, another character comes forward who has been listening and silent this whole time.

This character has not made any comment, or offered any argument, made no defence, nor put forward any opinion... until now. We actually had no idea he was there. But suddenly he stands up and speaks. Suddenly we see that the one that everyone had been talking about, had been there, quietly present, sitting shiva with Job all along. It is God who speaks.

Almighty and always present

And now God has something to say. Suddenly we are aware that God is not a far off. He is not talking from the throne room in Heaven where we met him before. Now is he is talking with Job face to face.

We can fall into the assumption, like Job's friends, of "either/or" God is either mighty and sovereign... like a king presiding in Heaven... far off and remote, OR he is like a friend who is present; and then we assume he is must also be quite impotent.... human and fallible.

But now we are introduced to a mysterious conundrum. The conundrum of 'AND'. God is the almighty sovereign one... AND he is God who is always present. Not either/or, but AND. Both dimensions are possible. Strength *and* love. Power *and* compassion. Just *and* merciful. Almighty *and* always present – side by side... together.

How do I sit with that mysterious conundrum that God is both/and... sovereign and love?

God has the last word

In all of this struggle and debate and wrestling, God has the last word. It is almost like we hold our breath… we want to hear the final word that may settle all of those unknowns in Job's heart. Now he might get to have his great, tormenting "Why?" question answered. Now he might be able to make sense of what hasn't made sense to him before

So, let's look at what God has to say…

Bible Reading
Job 38:1-27

God is the great Creator

This speech of God is one of my favourite passages of scripture. It is magnificent and beautiful! The astounding supremacy and strength of God's creative genius cannot be comprehended. We witness the stunning authority demonstrated in his creation with awe and we marvel at the work of his hand. If we read on, we see God chooses awe-inspiring examples of his creative genius…

>   The stealth of the lioness
>   The agility of the wild goats
>   The freedom of feral donkeys
>   The unruly raw strength of the wild buffalo
>   The impractical elegance of the adorned ostrich
>   The fierce glory of the battle stallion
>   The fearless flight of the formidable eagle

The majestic might of the One would create all of this, leaves us without words.

We can only bear witness to it... and it is appropriate to pause and acknowledge that God is the great creator.

When I think of remarkable creations in our world... what inspires me?

God converses in the storm

The playwright shows God talking and conversing with Job from out of a violent storm. A storm is such powerful imagery! In Australia are familiar with the power of violent storms and cyclones. Gale force wind that rips trees from the ground, and twists strong metal pylons like pretzels and launches sheets of iron like guillotines. Water that gushes and turns everything upside down, and leaves nothing as it was before. Force that leaves everything torn, and changed, and marked. We almost expect that God would speak from with-in the power of a storm. We feel its majesty and strength and power.

The God who is portrayed by Eliphaz, Bildab, Zophar and Elihu was the God of the storm... Almighty, powerful, awesome and strong. And the God who leaves in His wake horrifying devastation. Isn't this type of storm exactly what Job was going through? His life was cyclonic and chaotic... it was a violet storm. Everything was turned upside down and nothing was as it was before.

But sometimes I think that we can mistakenly fail to discern the difference between what God is bearing witness to, and what is his own voice. I wonder if God is letting Job know, that even in the power of the storm, God is there with him. God speaks from within the storm to let us know... His creative power is still supreme, still greater than the problems and the pain, still part of who God is. God knows what is happening... and that He is with us in the storm, and He is still in control. God is still sovereign.

God confronts Job directly

And then, at the end of this magnificent speech, God speaks directly to Job:

Bible Reading
Job 40:1-5

Here is a direct confronting challenge. And the challenge is this: Can the created, put the Creator on trial? Can the vessel charge the master-potter guilty of neglect... or worse... of grievous bodily harm?

Job answers this direct question. "I'm speechless," he responds. "I've spoken out of turn about things I didn't understand. I need to talk less and listen more." What an appropriate response to a powerful challenge.

Then God continues with another grand speech...

Bible Reading
Job 40:6-24
Job 41:1-34

The Presence of God

God's creatures are spectacular. This next speech is quite remarkable. God has spoken about common marvels – like the wild oxen, and the battle stallion with raw power and beauty we can appreciate. Things we are familiar with, and yet still we marvel at them.

The Behemoth and Leviathan

Now God takes time to consider two lesser-known creatures... creatures that inspire fear and terror. One from the land and one from the sea: The Behemoth and the Leviathan

Most commentaries believe the descriptions of these creatures refer to the hippopotamus and the crocodile. Formidable creatures yes... animals high on the food chain. But I wonder... what if... given the ancient timestamp of this text, what if the writer is referring to incredible creatures that they were familiar with during their time, but which are now extinct? Creatures that now only hold legendary status in our minds and have been relegated to fable in our contemporary culture.

"Grazing on grass, docile as a cow—"
"Strength of his back, the powerful muscles of his belly".
"His tail sways like a cedar in the wind; his huge legs are like beech trees."

This does not sound like a hippopotamus to me. I have seen a hippopotamus, and it didn't have a 'tail like a cedar tree'.

Then there is the Leviathan... a sea-creature that is wild and unruly... horrifyingly powerful and fearsome. We are familiar with crocodiles in Queensland and the Northern Territory. So, we know what a crocodile looks like. Could it be these interpretations are looking at these descriptions, through the lens of our limited experience? Older commentaries stick with the hippopotamus and crocodile interpretations... yet as formidable as they are, I personally think a dinosaur is a higher level of 'awe-inspiring'. We know dinosaurs existed – we have fossil evidence of that. What if this ancient literature is actually bearing witness to ancient creatures that they knew about?

Of course, we cannot say this for certain... but, for me, this seems to fit the intent of the passage with a little more ease than a hippopotamus... or a crocodile.

So, if you can allow that... be amazed that God's creation is truly spectacular: powerful, diverse and magnificent. However, if that seems too far-fetched to comprehend, we can still acknowledge God's creation is mind-blowingly incredible, including the remarkable fierce strength of the hippopotamus and crocodile.

God is supreme

These powerful examples of created wildlife are given to illustrate to a particular significant point: God is supreme; he created everything... including these fearsome creatures. These creatures cannot be tamed. God made them and they do not answer to humanity. How much more is God not answerable to humans.

Isaiah understood this:

> **Bible Reference**
> Isaiah 29:16

Isaiah uses the metaphor of the pottery house: We are not the potter. We are actually the clay... on the potter's wheel... being formed into beautiful creations... yes... but we do not tell the potter what to do. The potter does not need to explain himself. God is not accountable to the clay.

Job is learning this same principle here. The God who created the Behemoth and the Leviathan, also created us. We are to hold our Creator God with reverence and holy awe.

God sits in the silence with Job

But what is remarkable, is that in all of this demonstration of power and supremacy... we find something else that is quite remarkable. This time God has spoken to Job from the eye of the storm. Not the fury... but the calm, and the stillness.

> *I remember what the eye of the cyclone was like. I remember how I felt as the eye of Cyclone passed directly over us. I had a splitting headache, and I found out later that was attributed to the unusual low atmospheric pressure of that extreme weather event.*
> *I remember the quiet.*
> *I remember after all the fury... there was this eerie calm.*
> *Not a breath of a breeze.*
> *It was such a relief...*
> *A place to catch our breath, because we knew it was going to start all over again as soon as it the eye of the storm passed over.*

It was out of the calm and the stillness of the eye of the storm, that God speaks to Job. God speaks to him directly... close-up and personal. Job had his friends join him in the ashes. And now we see that God is there with him also, in the midst of the storm, literally... right in the middle of it... God is there.

And then we see God parts the storm to create a quiet place to speak honestly with Job. I notice that the storm isn't explained. We find that the "why" question is never addressed or explained. It remains unanswered.

We also notice that the storm isn't redirected. The storm isn't dissipated. The storm isn't supernaturally lifted up and taken somewhere else. The storm is still present. The storm is still going on. But in that storm, in the quiet of the eye, there is a still place... and that is where God is able to be with Job in a way that he can hear.

Do you remember... right at the beginning when Job first started to process all that had happened...

One of the deep cries in his heart... was his inability to access peace in the fury of his storm...

Bible Reading
Job 3:24-26

And yet here, God is creating a place of peace; of quietness; of rest. Peace seems impossible, given the force of the storm. Yet it is right here... accessible... available... and this is the place God creates for us, as he is with us in the storm. This eye-of-the-storm is not one that passes over and is gone while the storm rages on with more fury than it did before. No... this place of peace is always available to us. We can position ourselves in God's peace... any time, all the time.

So how does the playwright resolve and conclude the story of Job?

Bible Reading
Job 42: 1-17

Spoken in error

God clearly communicates that Eliphaz and his friends have spoken in error. Their legal lens, their projecting and patronising, their inability to truly listen, and spiritualising was not communicating the truth about God. The way they spoke was not representing God accurately. Their error was that they had misrepresented God terribly. And God calls them to account for that.

But did you notice that God doesn't throw Job's friends out... or discard them, for all of their terrible carry-on? They also have their own journey of experiencing mercy, grace and restoration. Job plays a significant role in this, through intercession and prayer.

I also notice that God was very okay with Job's honesty. Job was not judged for his cries of anguish. Or his candid confusion. Or his drowning doubt. This was *not* seen by God as sinful, or disrespectful, or unspiritual, or anti-Christian. It was an authentic cry of his heart... and God was with him in those places, the whole time.

It was also through those dark places that Job came the greatest revelation of his life:

Bible Reading
Job 42:5

Suffering was not a test

I think we understand fairly clearly now that Job's suffering was not punishment. But was it a test? Was it to see if Job could hold out, persevere and get through it? Sort of like an intense endurance event of the extreme kind? Would he cross the finish line?

No... this was not a test.

Remember the Accuser? It was the Accuser who was after evidence and wanted proof... not God. Our God is the God of unconditional love... without exception. What Job went through, was a storm... violent and destructive and horrific. Yet God was still sovereign and present. God was still loving him... without provisos and conditions.

Do I think of life as a test to pass?

Does anything change if we think about my relationship with God as a friend who sits shiva with me through my storms?

This means something else as well. If Job's circumstances and suffering were not a test, this also means that Job's restoration was not a reward.

Huh. It was not a case of – "You got through this, you persevered, you won... and your reward is that I will restore all that you had before, plus more..." There was nothing deserved or earned or gained. Job's restoration was not a prize for surviving. That style of thinking turns

God's love and generosity conditional, with stipulations that we have to meet. We have to achieve a mark of 50% or more, to pass.

God's sovereignty is loving mystery

Job's restoration was an expression of God's grace and unconditional love. His inventory after this, was doubled what he had started with. What was impressive and influential before, is now doubly impressive and influential. But it was not a not earned, not deserved... but God gave it anyway.

That's difficult, because... actually... I want Job to deserve this. I want him to be rewarded for surviving the pain and the barrage of terrible counsel. But as I have taken time to sit with this reality of God's generous grace... I find I am encouraged.

This makes Job's story like the rest of our stories. God is magnificent, and glorious, and marvellous... and there is *nothing* any of us can ever do to 'earn our way' to overcome, or to work through life's storms to have God bless us. Nothing...
Nothing.

Yet God shows us that he is here with us in the storm, creating a place of peace, with his love, and his grace, and his mercy to restore and bless us as well, in abundant and generous ways.

But let's not fall into the trap of thinking that we deserve it... or have earned it. God owes us nothing, but we owe God our very lives.
This is a mystery to us. That mysterious conundrum re-emerges. God who is powerful *and* loves us unconditionally... sovereign *and* gracious.

I think we still can have this tendency, like Eliphaz and Bildab, to hold up those legal scales and scrutinised the balance and project our worldly wisdom onto our understanding of our sovereign, creator God. Yet God says... my ways are higher than your ways...

My thoughts are higher than your thoughts. I love you with an everlasting love...

Bible Reference
Isaiah 55:8-9
Jeremiah 31:3

God is mystery. He speaks, in the eye of the storm, to tell us... "I am sovereign; I am almighty; I am always present; I am love; I am yours... and you are mine; And now your eyes have seen me."

Meister Eckhart was a German Franciscan monk in the 12th century, who went from being a highly respected teacher, to being brought before the inquisition for teaching heresy. He died being accused of misrepresenting God (– which is what heresy is...) in terrible ways. Yet much of Meister Eckhart's gentle work was around supporting ordinary people to find God accessible... in the rough storms of their lives. He is famous for preaching and teaching in the lay German language of the people – rather than teaching in Latin.
Meister Eckhart wrote this:
"Spirituality is not to be learned by flight from the world, or by running away from things, or by turning solitary and going apart from the world.
Rather, we must learn an inner solitude wherever or with whom-so-ever we may be.
We must learn to penetrate things and find God there."
Another famous quote of his:
"Nothing in all creation is so like God as stillness."
Doesn't this sound like the wisdom of Job?

What struck me most when I was reading about this man, was that it took 600 years for Meister Eckhart's life work to be recognised posthumously as legitimate theology. In his lifetime, he never got to see the storm pass over.

Like Job – Meister Eckhart was accused of misrepresenting God. He was commanded to repent, yet he maintained his innocence. Even in the storm of an inquisition, he was a person who understood how to be present with God in the stillness of the eye of the storm.

But unlike Job, Meister Eckhart never got to see a restoration, nor a vindication, nor any sense of justice achieved. His story didn't end like Job with a double inventory of stuff. Yet just because he didn't see that restoration, this doesn't make his story less profound. He wasn't less loved by God, but God chose to move differently in and through his story.

Perhaps Meister Eckhart's work is more famous, more influential than it might have been, because of this 'rediscovery' of the man and his writings, and what he went through.

So, leaving the results to God, Meister Eckhart firmly held onto the truth of God that he knew, the One he had seen in stillness of the storm. Meister Eckhart recognised that life is full of storms, and he lived with a genuine faith, that does not put all our energy into outrunning the storm, or avoiding the storm, or subduing it, but rather facing it, and engaging with it, and in that place... finding God. Finding the stillness of his presence.

Final thoughts...

Hearing God's voice, in the eye of the storm. Seeing God face to face. That is the place that leads us closer to God's heart.

Jesus said this very same thing:
During the last supper, on the eve of the greatest storm of his life, Jesus speaks this to his disciples in the upper room.

Bible Reference
John 14:27

In the storm of trouble, our hearts can naturally default to fear or intimidation or anguish or even paralysis... yet Jesus invites us into the eye of the storm. Into a place of peace that defies the fury of the tempest. A peace that is not like anything that the world offers.

The world would suggest that the storm must go away or be subdued for any sort of peace to be possible. But Jesus says, "I give you my peace... even from within the storm".

This is the miracle we witness in the story of Job. That in all of the fury of the storm, he found God... and he found peace. What a wonderful invitation for us to be present with God in this same way during our storms. What a wonderful invitation for us to be present with others during their storms... to be carriers of peace into the most tumultuous places.

Prayer:

Father God, we acknowledge that life can be full of the most violent storms. Yet you invite us to be still, and to hear your voice in the midst of the storm from a place of peace, when all of the world is turned upside down. Thank you that you are here... creating that place of calm for us. Thank you that you are sovereign, and you hold all things in your mighty hand... and you are always present. Father, we pray a blessing of peace over the people that we know who are going through storms. We also pray Father that we would be carriers of your peace into our families, into our workplaces, into our communities...
In Jesus Name, Amen.

Other books in this Series

Endnotes

ⁱ https://www.britannica.com/topic/The-Book-of-Job

ⁱⁱ https://biblescripture.net/Job.html

ⁱⁱⁱhttps://www.sparknotes.com/lit/oldtestament/section11/page/2

^{iv} Machine Gun Preacher is a 2011 American biographical action-drama film directed by Marc Forster and starring Gerard Butler, Michelle Monaghan; Distributed by Relativity Media, Starz Entertainment, Lionsgate Films.

^v https://answersingenesis.org/is-the-bible-true/book-of-job-fact-or-fiction/#fn_12

^{vi} CS Lewis – The Problem of Pain p90–1

^{vii} https://www.chabad.org/library/article_cdo/aid/370617/jewish/The-Rules-of-Shiva.htm

^{viii} Kruger, C. Baxter. Jesus and the Undoing of Adam.

^{ix} Masters Ph.d., Robert Augustus. Spiritual Bypassing: When Spirituality Disconnects Us from What Really Matters (p. 2). North Atlantic Books. Kindle Edition.

www.ingramcontent.com/pod-product-compliance
Lightning Source LLC
Chambersburg PA
CBHW052108070526
44584CB00017B/2388